Sue   £4

The Midland Around London

A COLOUR PORTFOLIO

KEVIN McCORMACK

Ian Allan
PUBLISHING

Previous page: A Bognor Regis-bound Southern 'HAL'/'BIL' electric unit from Victoria races Northampton-based Stanier 'Black Five' No 45292 at Salfords, north of Gatwick Airport. The Midland train is an excursion to Brighton, composed largely of Gresley London & North Eastern Railway (LNER) stock. *Kenneth Wightman*

Above: Euston's top-link shed, Camden, is full of diesels on 28 June 1962, but imminent Royal Train duty is being entrusted to 'Coronation' Pacifics Nos 46240 *City of Coventry* (leading) and 46244 *King George VI* (the standby locomotive). *Geoff Rixon*

Introduction

This latest album in the 'Colour Portfolio' series is a companion volume to *The Southern around London* and *The Western around London*, published by Ian Allan in 2003 and 2004 respectively, and covers the London Midland Region (LMR) of British Railways from the mid-1950s to the mid-1960s, when steam in the London area was eliminated. Although most of the pictures are of steam locomotives, some examples of diesel and electric traction from that period are also included. Indeed, some of the suburban electric units were considerably older than most of the steam locomotives running at that time.

For most enthusiasts reference to the LMR in the London area during the latter days of steam probably conjures up passenger services operating on the ex-London & North Western Railway (LNWR) line into and out of Euston, hauled by glamorous express locomotives designed for the London, Midland & Scottish (LMS) Railway: 'Princess Coronations' ('Duchesses'), 'Princess Royals', 'Royal Scots', 'Patriots' and 'Jubilees'. However, the

First published 2008

ISBN (10) 0 7110 3296 3
ISBN (13) 978 0 7110 3296 5

© Kevin R. McCormack 2008

Published by Ian Allan Publishing

an imprint of Ian Allan Publishing Ltd, Hersham, Surrey KT12 4RG
Printed in England by Ian Allan Printing Ltd, Hersham, Surrey KT12 4RG

Code: 0807/B

Visit the Ian Allan Publishing website at www.ianallanpublishing.com

ex-Midland Railway line serving St Pancras is also covered, as are some of the more prosaic services. Examples of the latter include inter-regional passenger and goods trains, suburban electric services, branch-line trains and other services for which the LMR provided motive power, such as those on the former Great Central main line out of Marylebone, the North London line to Richmond, the London, Tilbury & Southend line from Fenchurch Street and London Transport services beyond Rickmansworth on the former Metropolitan Railway ('the Met'). Consequently there are photographs of LMR locomotives at various 'foreign' locations around the capital.

During the period covered by this book I lived in Ealing, West London (Western Region territory), and I remember in 1958, when I was 11, hearing from a fellow locospotter at Ealing Broadway that if I wanted to see something different I should cycle over to Harlesden on the West Coast main line (WCML) out of Euston, because it wasn't that far from Ealing. I had only to get across Hanger Lane (this being before the gyratory system was built) and cycle past the Guinness Brewery, Park Royal goods yard, Central Middlesex Hospital and through the trading estate to Acton Lane; when I reached Harlesden I would find an open gate on the north side of the overbridge with a set of steps which provided an excellent vantage-point for the main line. If I turned around I could even see the mysterious line which crossed over the WCML and which carried inter-regional traffic hauled by particularly interesting locomotives. If I got bored I could cross the road and watch *Ergon*, the saddle tank, shunting among the wooden cooling towers at Acton Lane power station.

A few years later, when I started cycling to Old Oak Common locomotive shed, I was tipped off that Willesden shed was only a stone's throw beyond and less risky to get around. Willesden offered a wonderful variety of locomotives to see and photograph, whether in the roundhouse, repair works or in and around the running shed. I almost became a Midland convert!

It will be apparent from the historic images in this book that it is more than just the motive power that has changed dramatically over the years. The WCML electrification of the mid-1960s, with its associated overhead equipment and structures, has transformed (one might say æsthetically ruined) many of the scenes depicted in this book, and even locations with no overhead electrification are scarcely recognisable today, with the sole exception, perhaps, of Kew Gardens station (page 67). Furthermore, locomotive sheds have disappeared, while stations have been rebuilt and branch lines closed. Fortunately we can still enjoy the sight of large numbers of ex-LMS steam locomotives working on preserved railways, whilst a select number can even be seen operating specials on the national network. We should be particularly grateful to the holiday-camp operator, Sir Billy Butlin, who saved from the scrapyard four LMS express locomotives — *Royal Scot*, *Duchess of Hamilton* (both of which, incidentally, had been exhibited in North America), *Duchess of Sutherland* and *Princess Margaret Rose* — as well as four Southern tank engines (three Class A1X 'Terriers' and a Class B4 dock shunter).

In terms of the geographical coverage of this album, most of the views have been taken within a 25-mile radius of the capital, but a few are further afield, *e.g.* Bedfordshire and north Buckinghamshire. With regard to picture content, I should like to pay tribute to all the photographers listed below, whose historic colour material, believed to be previously unpublished, has formed the basis of this album: Geoff Rixon, Michael Allen, Bruce Jenkins, Jim Oatway, Nick Lera, Neil Davenport and Roy Hobbs. Photographs by Marcus Eavis, Ken Wightman, Frank Hunt and Dick Riley are reproduced courtesy of the Online Transport Archive, David Clark, Roger Jones (Light Railway Transit Association) and Rodney Lissenden respectively; photographs by Major Cotton are from the collection of Alan Sainty and my own.

Finally, I hope that readers will enjoy the pictures in this book, which, for many of us, will serve as a reminder of carefree days of youth spent at the lineside or visiting locomotive sheds watching the LMR at work, in blissful ignorance of the fact that everyday sights which we took for granted would shortly disappear for ever.

Kevin R. McCormack
Ashtead, Surrey
April 2008

Above: In appearance reminiscent of the LNWR 'Claughtons' and LMS unrebuilt 'Royal Scots', 'Patriot' No 45544 approaches Willesden Junction with a southbound fitted freight on 16 April 1960. This locomotive was one of only 11 unnamed examples of the class of 52. The first 42 were nominally rebuilds of 'Claughtons', but only the first pair actually incorporated parts from locomotives of this class. *Geoff Rixon*

Right: The last ex-LNWR locomotives to remain in service were the 'G2' and 'G2a' heavy-freight machines (generically called 'Super Ds', despite this referring originally to the earlier 'D' class after being superheated). The 'G2a' class consisted of rebuilds between 1936 and 1947 of Bowen-Cooke 'G1' locomotives introduced in 1912, an example of which, No 49078, is seen here at Willesden shed in April 1960. *Geoff Rixon*

Above and right: BR's modern 1960s image is portrayed in these two views from March 1967 and March 1966 respectively. In the first a DMU working to Broad Street and an EMU on the North London line (heading away from the camera) meet at Camden Road; in the second, at Watford Junction, main-line electrification has arrived, and a new electric locomotive, 'AL6' (Class 86) No E3111, in the short-lived 'Electric blue' livery, is seen hauling a Birmingham New Street–Euston service, although the livery of its carriages and the freight stock in the background still recall the steam era. *Marcus Eavis / Online Transport Archive (both)*

World War 2 delayed plans for the quadrupling of LT's lines beyond Harrow-on-the-Hill (shared with the LNER's services from Marylebone) and for extending electrification beyond Rickmansworth. Steam-operated passenger services on LT continued until 9 September 1961, and this view from 1957 depicts a Baker Street train waiting in the bay platform at Aylesbury behind Fairburn Class 4 tank No 42249. *Marcus Eavis / Online Transport Archive*

8

Right: Entering Euston's Platform 4 on 25 May 1960 hauling a local train is 'Crab' 2-6-0 No 42885, the epithet referring to the locomotive's ungainly appearance. Although built by the LMS between 1926 and 1932, the 245 mixed-traffic locomotives of this class were of pre-Grouping Lancashire & Yorkshire Railway appearance, having been designed by George Hughes, formerly of that company, after his appointment to the LMS. Note the seating available on Platform 2/3 for engine spotters, who are instructed not to pass beyond the board. *Major Cotton / Alan Sainty collection*

Right: Once the pride of the Southern Region, having been used regularly on the 'Golden Arrow' boat train, 'Britannia' No 70004 *William Shakespeare* looks somewhat jaded as it enters Euston station's Platform 1 in August 1962, under the watchful gaze of the regular crowd of locospotters. *Frank Hunt / LRTA collection*

This unique view from the fire escape of the Rotax factory in Harlesden depicts Stanier Class 5MT ('Black Five') 4-6-0 No 45113 hauling a breakdown train over the former Midland Railway line from Cricklewood to Acton Wells Junction (the mysterious line to which reference is made in the Introduction) on 14 May 1965. *Major Cotton / Alan Sainty collection*

Great Western Railway (GWR) influence, arising from Stanier's time at Swindon, was evident in many LMS designs, not least in his class of 40 mixed-traffic 2-6-0s built in 1933/4. One such locomotive, No 42947, is seen passing Watford shed with a ballast train on 26 May 1963.
Michael Allen

Above: No 44440, one of 580 Fowler Class 4F locomotives constructed between 1924 and 1940 and based on an earlier Midland Railway design, coasts into King's Langley station on 30 July 1960 at the head of a Bletchley–Euston local. Although these were primarily freight locomotives, their use on passenger turns was not uncommon. *Geoff Rixon*

Right: Pride of the LMS were the Stanier 'Princess Coronation' Pacifics. In this view from July 1963 No 46245 *City of London* and No 46240 *City of Coventry* rest inside Camden shed, two months before it closed to steam and its remaining allocation of 'Coronations' transferred to Willesden. Of the 38 members of this class 24 were originally streamlined, including these two locomotives. At the time of writing (April 2008) No 46229 *Duchess of Hamilton* is having its streamlined casing reaffixed. *Geoff Rixon*

Constructed in no fewer than 11 different workshops, by all four post-Grouping railway companies as well as by external builders, the Stanier '8F' 2-8-0s constituted one of the largest classes of main-line locomotive to be built in Britain. Of an overall total of 852, 666 ended up in BR ownership, including 42 ex-War Department locomotives repatriated from abroad. This view features No 48185, completed by North British in April 1942, heading a transfer freight near Stratford, on the Eastern Region. *Kenneth Wightman*

After initial restrictions, English Electric Type 4 diesel-electrics were
granted widespread route availability on main-line services from Euston
in July 1959, heralding the gradual replacement of steam on express
passenger trains in the run-up to electrification. On 3 October 1959
No D217 climbs Camden Bank on its way to Manchester. *R. C. Riley*

Left: This spotless, fully lined-out Stanier 'Black Five', No 45253, makes a fine sight as it hauls a southbound passenger train on the St Pancras line near Elstree in March 1962. The class totalled 842 machines, this example being completed by Armstrong Whitworth in September 1936. *John Cramp*

Right: By contrast, No 46220 *Coronation* has fallen on hard times. Under the watchful eyes of the locospotters who regularly occupied the north end of Platforms 2/3 at Euston station, this one-time holder of the world speed record is suffering the indignity of hauling a local train. The honour was earned by the locomotive on 29 June 1937, when it achieved 114mph, but was short-lived, the LNER's *Mallard* Pacific attaining 126mph on 3 July 1938. *Bruce Jenkins*

Right: In the years leading up to the arrival of William Stanier in 1932 the LMS was struggling to come up with a suitable type of modern passenger locomotive. After borrowing a GWR 'Castle' (but failing to obtain the drawings) in 1926 and then acquiring the drawings of the Southern's 'Lord Nelson' class, Stanier's predecessor Sir Henry Fowler produced his own 4-6-0 design, the parallel-boilered 'Royal Scot'. Stanier later rebuilt the 'Scots' with taper boilers, as shown here on No 46101 *Royal Scots Grey*, seen leaving Euston on 23 June 1962. *Bruce Jenkins*

Left: Little more than 10 years old and once the pride of Glasgow's Polmadie shed, 'Britannia' Pacific No 70052 *Firth of Tay* has been reduced to hauling a four-coach Nottingham Victoria–Marylebone semi-fast, being seen thus between Northolt Park and Sudbury in December 1965. The Great Central line was never a commercial success and, having arrived late on the scene (the London extension not being opened until 1899), was unable to compete with the longer-established railway companies such as the LNWR. *Author*

Right: Willesden motive-power depot, as seen from the towpath of the Grand Union Canal in April 1964, with 'Jinty' 0-6-0 tank No 47501 (on a separate siding) flanked by Stanier Class 8F No 48124 and, with its distinctive red nameplates, 'Royal Scot' No 46148 *The Manchester Regiment*. The running shed, seen on the right, was built in 1873. The depot would close completely on 27 September 1965. *Author*

The LMR took control of the former Great Central Railway line in 1958 and was able to stamp out any remaining competition from this route, with the result that main-line services were withdrawn with effect from

3 September 1966. This view from December 1963 features Stanier 'Black Five' No 44848 departing Marylebone with a train for Nottingham Victoria. *Marcus Eavis / Online Transport Archive*

Kentish Town was the passenger-locomotive depot serving St Pancras (Cricklewood being the goods shed), and on 15 April 1961 two Fowler Class 4 2-6-4 tanks, Nos 42342 and 42343, are seen near the coaling stage. This class of 125 locomotives was introduced in 1927, later examples differing from those shown here through having side-window cabs. *Jim Oatway*

The LNWR undertook a massive suburban electrification project, introducing electric services between Willesden Junction and Earl's Court via Addison Road (now Kensington Olympia) in 1914,

Broad Street and Richmond in 1916, and Watford and Euston in 1922. A set of Oerlikon open saloon stock dating from 1915-23 waits at Wembley Central in 1957. *Marcus Eavis / Online Transport Archive*

Following the untimely death in 1945 of Stanier's successor, Charles Fairburn, H. G. Ivatt became Chief Mechanical Engineer of the LMS, duly retaining this post with BR's London Midland Region. One of his designs was the Class 2 Mogul, which numbered 128 locomotives and was the inspiration for the later BR Standard '78xxx' class. This view features Ivatt No 46431 of Watford shed collecting goods vans at Hemel Hempstead station. *Geoff Rixon collection*

For many years the Bedford–St Pancras suburban services had an image problem (mainly for unreliability and overcrowding), contributing to the adoption of the line's derisory 'Bedpan' nickname. The appalling external appearance of comparatively new Standard Class 4 No 75038, seen at Bedford Midland in 1959 on a St Pancras train, hardly helps the cause; a small area on the cab side reveals how smart this locomotive could so easily have looked. *Marcus Eavis / Online Transport Archive*

Another numerous LMS class was Fowler's standard ('Jinty') 0-6-0T
shunter, developed from earlier Midland Railway designs by Johnson.
Built between 1924 and 1931, the class numbered 422 locomotives, of
which No 47432 is seen performing station-pilot duties at Marylebone
on 26 August 1964. *Michael Allen*

In 1890 the LNWR opened a two-mile branch from Harrow & Wealdstone to Stanmore (renamed Stanmore Village in 1950), with an intermediate station at Belmont. However, passenger traffic suffered after 1932, when the Met opened its own station at Stanmore (nowadays part of the Jubilee Line), which provided an electrified direct route to London. Following closure to passengers of the line beyond Belmont in September 1952, passenger services to Belmont and freight services to Stanmore Village continued until October 1964. Visiting the original terminus on a railtour on 27 April 1958 is Stanier push-pull 0-4-4 tank No 41901. *Frank Hunt / LRTA collection*

Gunnersbury station (known as Brentford Road for the first two years of its existence) was built by the London & South Western Railway (LSWR) in 1869 on a new line linking Richmond to Addison Road (Kensington Olympia) via Shepherd's Bush and Hammersmith. Further link lines were built, and from 1894 to 1906 no fewer than five railway companies operated services through Gunnersbury — the LSWR, the GWR, the Met, the North London Railway and the Metropolitan District Railway. Long past its heyday, Gunnersbury in 1957 was a scene of dereliction, exacerbated by the fact that a tornado had ripped off the original platform roof in 1954. The train in this view is composed of LNWR electric stock, with bodies built by Metropolitan-Cammell. The first units, delivered in 1914, had electrical equipment made by Siemens of Germany, but the onset of World War 1 caused the LNWR to commission Oerlikon, in neutral Switzerland, to equip subsequent batches. *Marcus Eavis / Online Transport Archive*

Above: The power and majesty of the 'Princess Coronation' Pacifics is graphically portrayed in this view of No 46238 *City of Carlisle* pounding through King's Langley in June 1960 on a Euston–Glasgow express formed of 14 carriages. The break in the running plate was exclusive to former streamliners and the two Ivatt locomotives built postwar. *Geoff Rixon*

Right: Only four 'Black Fives' carried names, and they spent most of their lives in Scotland, being named after Scottish regiments. However, No 45154 *Lanarkshire Yeomanry* had been transferred south to Newton Heath depot (Manchester) by 26 April 1963, when it was photographed on shed at Willesden. *Geoff Rixon*

45154

Above: Rebuilt 'Jubilee' No 45736 *Phoenix* approaches Linslade Tunnel, near Leighton Buzzard, at the head of a Manchester–Euston express in July 1962. This locomotive was one of only two 'Jubilees' to be fitted with a larger boiler, the alterations taking place in 1942 and resulting in their becoming almost indistinguishable from the rebuilt 'Royal Scots' and 'Patriots' which followed. *Geoff Rixon*

Right: Passing a GWR lower-quadrant signal near West London Junction signalbox, Battersea, Stanier '8F' No 48319 is about to disappear beneath the Southern Region lines to Waterloo and Victoria as it hauls a southbound transfer freight along the erstwhile West London Extension Railway in May 1961. *Jim Oatway*

Left: There are trains and railwaymen but not a passenger to be seen in this early-1965 scene featuring Cravens-built DMUs. Close to the Midland Railway station at Luton, on the St Pancras main line (seen in the distance, on the left), Luton Bute Street had opened in 1858 and would close to passengers on 26 April 1965. The station served a cross-country line linking the LNWR branch from Leighton Buzzard to Dunstable with the Great Northern Railway (GNR) main line at Hatfield. *Marcus Eavis / Online Transport Archive*

Above: Once the terminus of two branch lines, St Albans Abbey station lost its services on the ex-GNR line from Hatfield in 1951, but the LNWR branch from Watford Junction, opened in 1858, survives. Electrified in 1987/8, the line benefits from the support of a strong local users' group. This view of a Derby Lightweight DMU at St Albans Abbey dates from 1966.
Marcus Eavis / Online Transport Archive

Stanier's Class 5 4-6-0s were extremely versatile machines with a wide route availability and were thus well suited to inter-regional passenger excursions, thus obviating the need to change locomotives. In this view Rugby-based No 44716 is heading a special for Margate along Southern Region metals (not on LT lines, despite the centre rail!) near Downs Bridge, Beckenham, in Kent. *Kenneth Wightman*

Pictured on 31 August 1957, Standard Class 4 tank No 80064 hurries a down local train past Hunton Bridge, just north of Watford. The class numbered 155, construction taking place between 1951 and 1957. Fifteen examples survive, including this one, built in 1953.
Kenneth Wightman

Above and right: These photographs of Stanier 'Black Five' No 44862 hauling a goods train through Harrow & Wealdstone on 29 June 1964 and 'Princess Coronation' No 46242 *City of Glasgow* backing out of Euston in March 1960 have a tragic connection — the death of 112 people and injuries to a further 340. On 8 October 1952 Harrow & Wealdstone station was the location of Britain's second worst railway disaster, resulting in the destruction of two locomotives, 'Jubilee'

No 45637 *Windward Islands* and 'Princess Royal' No 46202 *Princess Anne.* However, the third locomotive involved, *City of Glasgow* (a former streamliner), was deemed salvageable and was rebuilt; this included the fitting of a continuous running-plate to the buffer-beam, which thereafter distinguished it from the other 'de-streamlined' locomotives. *Michael Allen; Geoff Rixon*

In 1925 the Met electrified the line from Harrow-on-the-Hill to Rickmansworth, from where its own steam locomotives hauled the trains for the remainder of the journey to Aylesbury, Quainton Road and Verney Junction. In 1936, three years after the Met's absorption into LT, services were withdrawn beyond Aylesbury, the truncated non-electrified section being operated from 1937 on LT's behalf by the LNER and later by BR's London Midland Region. Fowler Class 4 tank No 42328 is seen about to couple up to an Aylesbury-bound train at Rickmansworth on 19 June 1954. *Neil Davenport*

On the same day Stanier 'Jubilee' No 45686 *St. Vincent* stands at Watford Junction at the head of a parcels train, the leading vehicle being of Hawksworth GWR design. The 'Jubilee' class numbered 191 locomotives, of which the first, as yet unnamed, entered service in 1934. The next 112 were also initially unnamed, but eventually, the whole class bore names, mainly associated with the British Empire or the Royal Navy. *Neil Davenport*

Left: Another view of the Cricklewood–Acton Wells Junction line (see page 10), this time between Neasden and Harlesden. A resplendent Fowler Class 3 tank, No 40031, fitted with condensing apparatus for working to Moorgate, approaches Craven Park on a railtour on 2 September 1961. *Michael Allen*

Above: Memories of Euston's Great Hall, destroyed along with the Doric Arch in the 1960s station-rebuilding project, are rekindled by the large signboard facing Platform 1 as Polmadie (Glasgow)-based 'Princess Coronation' No 46222 *Queen Mary* simmers at the buffer-stops after bringing in the 'Royal Scot' express in March 1960. *Geoff Rixon*

Above: By the time this photograph was taken late in 1965 through trains on the former Great Central main line were already in serious decline, justifying only four carriages. Stanier 'Black Five' No 44710, heading for Marylebone, is seen approaching the North Circular road (A406) overbridge at Neasden. The buildings to the right of the locomotive form part of the LT Underground depot. *Author*

Right: Maintaining the LT connection is Ivatt Class 2 No 41284, taking water at Chesham, on the Met. Opened in 1889, the branch from Chalfont & Latimer (originally Chalfont Road) to Chesham was worked by steam until 1960, when the line was electrified. LT had twice given serious consideration to 'dieselising' the line, first in 1936, when it ordered two AEC diesel railcars (similar to the GWR's 'Flying Bananas') only to cancel the order, and again in 1952, when it borrowed the ACV experimental three-car unit (see page 52). *Marcus Eavis / Online Transport Archive*

Left: Stanier's mixed-traffic 'Black Five' locomotives numbered 842 machines, built between 1934 and 1951 and containing a number of variants, including 22 rather ugly specimens fitted with Caprotti valve gear.
No 44748, from the main batch of 20 Caprotti locomotives with low running-plates and splashers, is seen piloting an unrebuilt 'Patriot' through Willesden Junction station in 1960. *Geoff Rixon*

Left: Class 3F 0-6-0 No 43325 of Watford shed passes through King's Langley station with a short van train in June 1960. This Midland Railway veteran had been one of a large number of Johnson Class 2 locomotives constructed in the period 1888-1902, many of which, including this example, were rebuilt (from 1916) with larger Class 3 boilers and Belpaire fireboxes. *Geoff Rixon*

Rebuilt 'Patriot' No 45512 Bunsen passes a Standard Class 5 as it moves around Willesden depot on 27 June 1964. Nos 45502-41 were nominally rebuilds of 'Claughtons', but this was no more than an accounting exercise, since they were entirely new locomotives, albeit originally allotted ex-Claughton numbers. *Major Cotton / Author's collection*

Above: A picture to confuse the unwary — a steam-hauled LMR commuter train arriving at a London terminus, but which one? The date is 1 March 1963, and the train is the 7.42am from Tring, hauled by Fairburn tank No 42071. The location is Broad Street, the former North London Railway station which used to stand next to Liverpool Street station. *Michael Allen*

Right: Action stations at Aylesbury Town as the pioneer BR Standard Class 5, No 73000, departs with the 2.38pm from Marylebone to Nottingham (Victoria) on 15 August 1964. This class was a development of the Stanier 'Black Five', the last two of which were fitted with high running-plates similar to that seen here. *Bruce Jenkins*

PASSENGERS MUST
CROSS THE LINE
BY THE BRIDGE

73000

Left: Opened in 1862, the 4½-mile branch from Watford Junction to Rickmansworth (later given the suffix 'Church Street') was electrified in 1927 to counter competition from the Met, which had a direct electric service to London from its own station at Rickmansworth. However, patronage continued to be poor, and passenger services ceased in March 1952, although regular freight services operated until 1966. On one such working 'Jinty' No 47355, crosses the River Chess as it approaches the terminus on 16 March 1962. The conductor rails had already been removed, but not the warning sign! *Nick Lera*

Right: On the same date Fowler Class 2P 4-4-0 No 40672 is seen leaving Watford shed. Unfortunately no examples of this class survive today; however, arising from the Midland Railway's acquisition in 1903 of the Belfast & Northern Counties Railway, 18 almost-identical 'U2'-class locomotives ran in Northern Ireland, and one of these — No 74 *Dunluce Castle*, dating from 1924 — is preserved in the Ulster Folk & Transport Museum in Belfast, appropriately in crimson-lake livery. *Nick Lera*

Left: 'Jinty' No 47501 steams into view as 'Royal Scot' No 46155 *The Lancer* pulls away from Willesden Junction station *c*1963. The first 50 'Royal Scots' had been built at the Glasgow works of the North British Locomotive Co, but this example was constructed by the LMS at Derby. *Geoff Rixon*

Below left: Rebuilt 'Royal Scot' No 46127 *Old Contemptibles* climbs Camden Bank in June 1962, passing the down side carriage sidings — and the decorated retaining wall upon which local residents insisted when the line was built in 1837. There was little to distinguish rebuilt 'Scots' from rebuilt 'Patriots' save that the former had a cutaway cab aperture and a sandbox mounted on the running-plate. *Bruce Jenkins*

Right: As electrification infrastructure creeps southwards, Stanier Class 4 2-6-4 tank No 42430 hurries a Euston–Bletchley train along the down main line at Berkhamsted in May 1964. *Geoff Rixon*

Starting in 1953, BR tried out a three-car ACV lightweight diesel unit on several branch lines in the London area. Having run initially in a livery of two-tone grey with red relief, it was repainted green in 1955.

In 1957 it was used on the St Albans Abbey branch, being seen here at Watford Junction with an LNWR 'Super D' 0-8-0 in the background.
Marcus Eavis / Online Transport Archive

The Watford Junction–Croxley Green branch opened in 1912, and electric services started in 1922. This shot of a brand-new electric unit was taken in the summer of 1957 at one of the intermediate stations, Watford West. Services on the branch ceased on 22 March 1996, but the line remains *in situ* in anticipation of its being connected to the Met, from north of the latter's Croxley station to Watford West (a short section into Croxley Green station has been severed by a road and would be abandoned); this link would enable Met trains which currently terminate at Watford (Met) to reach the West Coast main line at Watford Junction. *Marcus Eavis / Online Transport Archive*

Above: The 1.03pm from Woodford Halse to Marylebone was somewhat over-powered on this particular day in 1959 when photographed at Aylesbury Town. Piloting ex-LNER Class B1 No 61271 and seen taking on water is a 'Flying Pig', this being the nickname given to Ivatt's ugly design of Class 4 Mogul, which started to appear in the last month of the LMS's existence and by the end of 1952 numbered 162 examples. No 43063 was turned out by Doncaster Works in 1950. *Marcus Eavis / Online Transport Archive*

Right: Also in 1959 — before the station was re-sited — one of the non-condensing Fowler Class 3 2-6-2 tanks, No 40020, prepares to leave Bedford (St Johns) with the 3.55pm to Bletchley. This is the only section of the Oxford–Cambridge cross-country route to remain open today, although there are hopes that the entire line may one day be restored. *Marcus Eavis / Online Transport Archive*

Left: A Class 5 goes Underground! No 45217 brings the 7.20am Leicester Central–Marylebone train through LT's Chalfont & Latimer station on 9 September 1961. The opposite face of the island platform which the BR train is passing serves the Chesham branch. *Michael Allen*

Above: No glamour in this picture at Willesden depot, taken on 22 June 1963 — some three months before Camden depot closed and royalty in the form of 'Duchesses' arrived. Willesden's typical allocation of the time comprising engines for parcels, freight and empty-stock workings is represented here by Hughes 'Crab' No 42810, Fairburn tank No 42118, Stanier 'Black Five' No 44870 and Stanier Class 8F No 48665. *Michael Allen*

Having arrived from Aylesbury with a train for Baker Street, Fairburn tank No 42250 is seen prior to handing over to a Met electric locomotive at Rickmansworth station in 1961, shortly before the end of steam operation. Electrification to Amersham saw the replacement of the Met electric locomotives by A60 stock (still in operation today!) and the withdrawal of LT services to Aylesbury, which thereafter would be served exclusively by BR from Marylebone. *Marcus Eavis / Online Transport Archive*

After traversing the north side of the Gunnersbury triangle, a Brent–West Kensington freight headed by 'Jinty' 0-6-0 tank No 47432 waits for a clear road on the approach to LT's Turnham Green station on 2 June 1965. The train is standing on the up track of the original (1869) LSWR line from Kensington (Addison Road) to Richmond. The westbound Piccadilly Line is on the embankment behind; in the foreground is the westbound District Line to Richmond.
Nick Lera

Above: The flowers are blooming at Euston station in this view from Platform 1 of 'Princess Coronation' No 46251 *City of Nottingham* waiting to depart in July 1961. BR maroon livery, similar to that used by the LMS, was applied between December 1957 and November 1958 to 16 of this class of 38. *Jim Oatway*

Right: Fowler Class 3 2-6-2 tank No 40026 coasts along the Southern's electrified line between Clapham Junction and West London Junction signalbox, to the north of the carriage-washing plant located on the main line into Waterloo. The locomotive was one of 19 of this 70-strong class to be fitted with condensing apparatus for working through the tunnels to Moorgate. *Jim Oatway*

Left: The Midland Railway absorbed the London, Tilbury & Southend Railway in 1912, and in the latter years of steam most services were in the hands of powerful three-cylinder LMS Stanier 2-6-4 tanks, the entire class of 37 being allocated to Shoeburyness, in Essex. On 13 January 1962 No 42530 draws into Upminster station with the 1.07pm Fenchurch Street–Shoeburyness. *Michael Allen*

Above: With some Midland Railway lower-quadrant signals in evidence on the left of the picture, Stanier 'Jubilee' No 45667 *Jellicoe* heads the 12.12pm Derby–St Pancras between Cricklewood and West Hampstead on 2 September 1961. The class name was derived from numerically the first locomotive, No 5552 (but which was actually a newer locomotive, No 5642, renumbered!), named *Silver Jubilee* to commemorate the royal milestone reached by King George V and Queen Mary in 1935. *Michael Allen*

The 13 'Princess Royal' Pacifics — arguably enlarged GWR 'Kings' — were largely overshadowed by the later 'Princess Coronations' but were still highly successful on express passenger work. The pioneer locomotive, No 46200, which had been completed in June 1933 and gave its name to the class, was one of four to be painted maroon in the late 1950s. In this photograph, taken on 1 August 1960 at Hunton Bridge, it is providing unusual motive power for an inter-regional train composed of Maunsell SR stock. *Geoff Rixon*

Following the success of its diesel-electric shunters, introduced in 1932, the LMS decided to venture into building main-line diesel locomotives and before the onset of nationalisation began constructing two identical Co-Co diesel-electrics, Nos 10000 and 10001. However, only the former, on the extreme left of this interior view of Willesden's 1929-built roundhouse, was actually completed before the LMS's demise on 31 December 1947; when BR was formed its twin (centre) was still under construction at Derby Locomotive Works. On the right is a 'D8xxx' English Electric Type 1 diesel (nowadays Class 20), a remarkable design introduced in 1957 and which has now seen more than 50 years of main-line service. *Geoff Rixon*

'Royal Scot' No 46128 *The Lovat Scouts* arrives at Euston's Platform 1 in 1962 with a train from Manchester. This locomotive was one of the first 50 of the class, built in 1927 at the North British Locomotive Works in Glasgow, the remainder being constructed by the LMS at Derby in 1930. Originally carrying parallel boilers and resembling the unrebuilt 'Patriots', the 'Royal Scots' were all rebuilt with taper boilers between 1943 and 1955 (excluding No 46170, which, as LMS No 6399, had been rebuilt in 1935). *Geoff Rixon*

In 1925 increased passenger traffic arising from electrification prompted the LMS to order more electric units. To accelerate loading and unloading, compartment (rather than open-saloon) stock was ordered. Metropolitan-Cammell was again chosen to construct the bodywork, but electrical equipment was supplied by Metropolitan Vickers, owned by GEC. One such train is seen in 1957 at Kew Gardens, where the original station building dating from 1869 still stands today. Unusually the footbridge is even Grade II Listed. Designed by French engineer François Hennebique and built in 1912 in reinforced concrete, it featured high sides intended to protect passengers' clothes from smoke.
Marcus Eavis / Online Transport Archive

Above: To commemorate the Met's centenary, on 26 May 1963 LT ran a special composed of 'Dreadnought' locomotive-hauled stock (dating from 1912-23) between Baker Street and Aylesbury. For the final section beyond Amersham the LMR provided an unusual but sadly unkempt steam locomotive, 'Jubilee' No 45709 *Implacable*. This extraordinary vintage train is seen approaching Amersham on its return from Aylesbury. *Marcus Eavis / Online Transport Archive*

Right: In the years 1946-8 Ivatt had 18 'Patriot' locomotives rebuilt with double chimneys, new cylinders and large tapered boilers, among them No 45529 *Stephenson*, seen at South Kenton on 21 June 1963. The train is the unadvertised 2.08pm Euston–Liverpool Lime Street, first stop Crewe — a fast relief train which preceded the slower timetabled service. *Major Cotton / Author's collection*

Buckingham may seem busy in this 1959 view, but the diesel railcars introduced in August 1956 on the Banbury (Merton Street) –Buckingham section of line could not prevent the withdrawal of passenger services on 31 December 1960. Their subsequent transfer to the Buckingham–Bletchley section, represented here by Ivatt tank No 41275 on a push-pull train, was similarly insufficient to prevent the line's closure with effect from 5 September 1964 to passengers — with the exception of HM The Queen, who visited on 4 April 1966! *Marcus Eavis / Online Transport Archive*

Stanier Mogul No 42978 stands at Euston station on 24 April 1962, the narrowness of its Fowler tender being clearly evident. Although the Hughes/Fowler 'Crabs' represented a successful class, when 40 more Moguls were required in 1933 Stanier, who had just arrived from the GWR, decided that the additional locomotives should be built to his own design. *Major Cotton / Alan Sainty collection*

Above: Photographed during the last week of Western Region steam, at the end of December 1965, 'Black Five' No 44860 stands at Wooburn Green on the now-defunct line from High Wycombe to Bourne End. When the design was introduced by Stanier in 1934 the expectation was that the number series, which commenced at 5000, would reach no higher than 5499, the numbers from 5500 being allocated to the 'Patriot' and 'Jubilee' classes. However, with the ordering of further 'Black Fives' lower numbers had to be used, and (including the initial '4' added by BR) the series eventually ran from 44658 to 45499. The locomotive shown here was thus one of the later machines, completed in 1949 under the auspices of BR. *Author*

Right: Given special dispensation to operate this railtour on 14 April 1962, having just been withdrawn after running out of boiler time, Fowler '2P' 4-4-0 No 40646 hurries away from Dunstable towards Leighton Buzzard on the line from Luton (Bute Street), which was to close to passengers on 30 June. The last of these attractive locomotives would be withdrawn at the end of the year. *Roy Hobbs*

Left: The down 'Midland Pullman' passes St Albans shed in June 1961. Composed of a six-car diesel-electric unit (one of two allocated to the LMR for such work), this luxury train, the first on BR to be fitted with full air-conditioning, was introduced in July 1960, serving Leicester and Manchester from St Pancras.
Bruce Jenkins

Left: Three months earlier, more traditional motive power in the form of 'Jubilee' No 45575 *Madras* takes a train out of St Pancras. The LMS constructed the first of these locomotives in May 1934, but No 45575 was completed in September 1934 as part of a batch built by the North British Locomotive Co. Before the LMS decided to name one of the class *Silver Jubilee* in April 1935, they were known simply as Class 5XP.
Bruce Jenkins

In this rare daylight photograph Metropolitan Vickers Co-Bo diesels Nos D5717 and D5711 head away from Hendon with the overnight 'Condor' (Container Door to Door) express freight to Glasgow in July 1959. These locomotives (known latterly as Class 28) were particularly unreliable, and all 20 had been withdrawn by the end of 1968 after (at most) 10 years' service. *Bruce Jenkins*

Left: Unrebuilt and unnamed 'Patriot' No 45547 is viewed from a convenient wagon inside Willesden's running shed in April 1960. These locomotives were designed by Fowler as a lighter version of the 'Royal Scot' class, with wider route availability, to replace the inefficient 'Claughton' class, from which they were developed. *Geoff Rixon*

Above: From 1947 several experimental variants of the numerous 'Black Five' class were produced, including this example, No 44765, fitted with Timken roller bearings throughout and double chimney. The locomotive is pictured in unlined black livery at Willesden depot on 12 May 1965. *Major Cotton / Author's collection*

Above: St Albans City station, on the Midland Railway main line from St Pancras, was opened in 1868, 10 years after the LNWR reached St Albans via a branch line from Watford Junction on the West Coast main line from Euston (see page 33). In this view dating from 1959 No 43565, an elderly Johnson '3F' 0-6-0 rebuilt by Fowler with Belpaire firebox, trundles through at the head of a freight train.
Marcus Eavis / Online Transport Archive

Right: Stanier '8F' 2-8-0 No 48632, unusually paired with a Fowler tender, hauls a freight on the Hammersmith & Chiswick branch on 21 June 1962. Heading towards South Acton (Gatehouse Junction), having broken its journey from Willesden to Kew Bridge North Yard, it is pictured near the site of Rugby Road Halt. The sign refers to the Bath Road level crossing 1,360 yards away (there is a missing digit), over which the train has already passed, while the overgrown sidings in the foreground served the Napier Motor Works and Parry's coal wharf. The line would close completely on 3 May 1965, passenger services having been withdrawn as early as 1 January 1917. *Nick Lera*

Index of Locations

Front cover: The date is 19 September 1964, and 'Royal Scot' No 46155 *The Lancer* is about to depart St Pancras station with the 'Pennine Limited' railtour, organised by the Locomotive Club of Great Britain (LCGB). The 70 original members of the class were all rebuilt with Stanier taper boilers between 1943 and 1955. The 71st 'Royal Scot', formerly the high-pressure compound locomotive No 6399 *Fury*, had effectively joined the class back in 1935, when it was rebuilt as a 'simple' with a taper boiler to replace the original, which had exploded during trials. *Michael Allen*

Back cover: Watford shed's much-cherished Fowler 2P No 40672, built in 1928, awaits its next duty in 1957. For over 25 years from 1936, this locomotive served 'Engineer Watford', hauling the Inspection Saloon around the area. Peeping out of the shed is Ivatt Class 2 tank No 41320. *Marcus Eavis / Online Transport Archive*